Just Like
Watching Brazil

Ian McMillan

Yorkshire Art Circus
in association with
The Barnsley Chronicle

Published by **Yorkshire Art Circus** in association with the Barnsley Chronicle
School Lane
Glasshoughton
Castleford
WF10 4QH
Tel: 01977 550401
Fax: 01977 512819
e-mail: books@artcircus.org.uk
web: www.artcircus.org.uk

© Text: Ian McMillan
© Photographs: The Barnsley Chronicle

Support: Ian Daley, Isabel Galan, Lorna Hey

Thanks go to Keith Lodge of the Barnsley Chronicle, to Mark Jobst of the BBC
and to Michael Spinks and Chris Patzelt of Barnsley FC

Some of these poems first appeared in the Barnsley Chronicle, Perfect Pitch,
Better Red than Dead, Yorkshire Post and on the Today Programme, on BBC
Radio Four and Five and on Sky Sports

Cover Design: Paul Miller of Ergo Design
Printed by FM Repro, Liversedge

ISBN: 1 898311 41 2

Classification: Poetry/Sport

British Library Cataloguing in Publication Data.
A catalogue record for this book is available from the British Library.

Yorkshire Art Circus is a unique book publisher. We work to increase access to
writing and publishing and to develop new models of practice for arts in the
community.

Please write to us for details of our full programme of workshops and our
current book list. Our Website www.artcircus.org.uk
Yorkshire Art Circus is a registered charity No 1007443.

Yorkshire Art Circus is supported by:

Contents

After the Silence

26 April 1997
Barnsley 2 Bradford 0
4.47 pm, Final Whistle.

That moment of silence
before the roar
when all the bad news
trickled away
like water down a drain on Grove Street

That moment of silence
before the song
when real life seemed like
a shadow
beside a football at Neil Redfearn's feet

After the silence
the singing will come
after the silence
the dancing will come
after the silence
the tears will fall
after the silence
that covers all …

But savour
that moment of silence
when time stands still
and the future pivots
on a Barnsley hill
and a town that's been beaten
and left for dead
has a smile on its lips
and a song in its head.

Premier Days

I've always woken up before the alarm clock; take that as a metaphor if you like, read it as an image of the ever-watchful writer, the eyes and ears of the tribe, but it's just a fact. I always wake up before the alarm clock. Except once.

Premiership fever was at boiling point last Summer in Barnsley; every car that passed had a sticker in the back, every time you turned to the back page of the Barnsley Chronicle you saw the smiling face of yet another close-season signing: George Hristov, the bewildered looking werewolf from Eastern Europe who was going to be our Juninho; Eric Tinkler, the huge South African who was simply going to stop them getting past him in midfield, and Lars Leese, the German goalkeeper, tall as a basketball player, who said he used to follow Barnsley on German TV. They all made us smile.

My job as poet-in-residence at the club was part of the maelstrom. The idea came to me and my mate, local head teacher and Barnsley fanatic Julian Wroe, in the Royal Oak in Wombwell one quiet Wednesday night. I'd worked a lot around Barnsley as a poet-in-the-community and being the poet at the football club seemed like a logical progression. We agreed to hold back on the publicity for a while and then do a proper press release at the start of the next season; at that time we weren't even promoted, and several nail-biting weeks lay ahead. I'm a fool: late in the Spring I was writing something for the Yorkshire Post and the features editor happened to ask me if I'd got anything else in the pipeline and I told him about the Barnsley FC job and he told a reporter and they printed a little bit on the front page one slow Monday about me being Barnsley's first Premiership signing, and then all hell broke loose. It started slowly and built up: Radio Ulster rang me, and I did a live interview; I wandered around on a mobile phone talking live to Alan Beswick on GMR, I was on Talk Radio twice in the same day and neither producer knew I'd been on the other show. I must have done thirty radio and TV interviews, and it's still carrying on. But I'm jumping the gun.

Premiership fever last Summer went hand-in-hand with Season Ticket Nerves. I didn't have a season ticket when we were in the First

Division mainly because I took varying amounts of kids. I've got three of my own and I sometimes took my late brother-in-law's two. Sometimes I took one child, sometimes five. But for the premiership we would all need season tickets, and word began to spread that they had all gone; that there were nine left; that there were thousands left; that they were going to build a new stand so that everybody could get in.

Then it was announced in the Barnsley Chronicle that after the existing Season Ticket holders had got theirs, and after the club lottery ticket holders had got theirs, then holders of ten ticket stubs from previous league games could get theirs. Ten ticket stubs: that means sixty stubs. I'd saved all mine and the kids saved all theirs. We made piles of them. Fifty-six. We dug in pockets and behind drawers. Fifty-eight. Then my wife pointed out that for ten ticket stubs you got two season tickets. So we only needed thirty. And we'd got fifty-eight. We were rich!

It was a strange, mad time to be in town; tales of huge queues at the box office were bandied around. All the season tickets would be gone before they got to the ten stubbers. All the season tickets had gone on the first day. There were never more than two hundred season tickets available.

As I said, I always wake up before the alarm clock. I went to bed ridiculously early on the Friday night before I had to go and queue for my season tickets. I set the alarm for four-thirty in the morning. I fell in and out of sleep, listening to 5 Live on my headphones. I knew that I would wake up before the alarm clock and so I switched it off. And I fell deeply asleep. And suddenly it was twenty past five, and it felt like the middle of the afternoon. I fell out of bed and got dressed.

I'll never forget that long, slow walk in the early morning mist. Three miles from my house to Oakwell. Up Tempest Avenue to the main Barnsley/Doncaster road. Along the road, past the pig farm and the curious cows. Across the valley, the hazy streetlights of Wombwell, and beyond that the darkness where Manvers coking plant used to be. Through Ardsley, past the crematorium and the student hall of residence that used to be an old people's home. There were lights on in a couple of the students' rooms; they couldn't be up already, surely? Barnsley never used to have a student population, just a few mining engineers at the tech, but now the popular music course at the College was attracting people from all over the country and there were indie band nights at some of the pubs. I began to walk more quickly now, and I began to sweat. As I bent to tie my shoelaces a bus went past. Still, it wasn't far to go. I'd be quite near the front of the season ticket queue, because nobody in Barnsley got up early these days.

I turned down the hill past the monumental masons; ahead of me were the Oakwell floodlights, and my heart began to beat a bit faster, like it always did. It was ten past six in the morning.

I got to the car park and stood there, just stood there. The car park was completely full, and I could see a snake of people from the box office, right round the walls of the club. There must have been two thousand people; men, women, children. Some were drinking beer, some were cooking breakfast on small stoves. A van rolled up selling bacon sarnies and cups of tea. A car full of coppers watched warily. I made my way to the back of the queue. People I knew waved at me. A man I sometimes saw on the bus said he'd been there since ten o'clock the previous night. I stood there. An old man stood behind me, and behind him stood a man with a chair. This was it: Barnsley in the Premiership, a town that had had years and years of terrible news was now queueing up for the good news. The Holy Grail: season tickets and a chance to play Manchester United instead of Port Vale. The old man behind me spoke, with a voice like gravel: 'Me and the wife are supposed to be going to see the Endeavour at Whitby at half past nine he said. 'I've come all the way from Hull' said the man with the chair. Funny thing, but he never sat on that chair all morning.

So we stood there, not moving, talking about games. About the great game when we got promoted, April 26th, beating Bradford two-nil, goals by Paul Wilkinson and Clint Marcelle, about the time we were all walking home through the car park when we heard that Wolves had been beaten in the sixth minute of extra time by Reading, and we all danced the conga round the cars. We talked about the coming season, about how we stood quite a good chance against a lot of the teams, about how there were two premierships and we might not be able to beat Liverpool but we could certainly beat Southampton.

Time passed, slowly. News filtered back that the box office had opened. A mobile phone rang. It was the old man's. He took it out of his pocket. 'That'll be the Ayatollah' he said. He held it too close to his mouth. 'Speak' he barked. We heard his wife's voice saying that it was half past nine and they should be going to Whitby to see the Endeavour. 'I'm on my own bloody endeavour here' he said, and we knew what he meant. The queue began to move, achingly slowly. Rumours flew and we tried to ignore them. A man three or four people behind me in the queue was counting his stubs, obsessively. 'Thirty stubs' he said, 'for six season tickets.' 'Like me' I said, 'I've got thirty.' 'They're mainly from the one game; I went round the seats picking 'em up sometime last winter. Good job I saved 'em.' There was a silence. The old man with the mobile phone spoke. 'You have to have 'em from ten different games' he said. The subsequent swapping passed some more time.

Someone came out of the box office with a policeman. The policeman shouted 'Will you all listen please! Will you all listen!'. The person from the box office's voice was quieter, but we got the gist: there were nearly three thousand of us in the queue, but they could only process eight hundred that day. The rest of us could either go home and come back to queue tomorrow or we could put our forms and our money and our kids' birth certificates and our late brother-in-law's kids' birth certificates in a numbered envelope and we'd be dealt with in order.

'Can we have a receipt?' someone shouted.

'No, but we'll staple the envelopes up' said the person from the box office.

So there we were, a microcosm of the history of northern life, trusting all our hopes and fears to someone with a box, watching our precious birth certificates and cash get stapled up. It was after dinner now, and I needed to go for the bus home. Still, at least we're in the premiership, I said to the man with the chair.

'Yes', he said; 'now the adventure can begin.' And the season stretched in front of us, holding all our dreams like you hold a precious ornament, or an ornament you've been told is precious. And I went home and waited for August.

Home Support

It is mid-July, 1997. It is hot.
Barnsley are in the Premier League,
and in my head our season
is laid out as simple as an Underground Map,
or a child's drawing of the solar system.
Mid-July, a pre-season friendly
against Doncaster. The start of something
and one of my daughters is coming to Doncaster
on her own for the first time on the bus
to meet me to go to the match. As the bus
rolls into the bus station I see her red shirt
upstairs, and she waves, and my heart breaks

for her, and me, and her red shirt with 21 TINKLER
on the back, and the bus driver who is a Middlesbrough fan,
and the other people who tumble off the bus in their red shirts
with the season laid out in their heads simple and lovely
as a map of the solar system or a child's drawing
of the Underground, and the Greek bus station toilet attendant
who knows me and shouts PREMIER LEAGUE, but
mostly it breaks for her, and me, and her red shirt.

Still, it's July. It's hot. We meet Chris and Duncan
and we try to go into a pub even though my daughter's
a bit young and a man in a suit says Sorry, Home Support Only.
And my heart breaks

for her, and me, and her red shirt, and the Home Support
who cheer Doncaster and whose season is laid out simple
as a serving suggestion, or a child's drawing of a football team,
but mostly it breaks for her and me.

We get a taxi home, which seems extravagant, but I think
of the Greek toilet attendant and I shout PREMIER LEAGUE
on our path as we walk into the house, father and daughter,
red shirt, hot night, Home Support, season laid out in our heads
simple and lovely as a football programme, simple and lovely
as a penalty kick, a well-taken corner.

Oakwell Sunrise

Oakwell sunrise,
Brand new era!
Place in Europe
getting nearer!

Danny's boys
in the Premiership,
Brace yourselves
for an exciting trip!

Oakwell sunrise,
brand new day,
see how the Barnsley
men can play!

Unforgettable season
about to begin
take a deep, deep breath
and dive straight in!

This is Where it Starts

This is the beginning of the great adventure,
This is the start of the dream;
This is where the future unfolds
For a premier football team.

The season's laid out like a street
where snow fell overnight
and you're waiting and eager to make your prints
and have a snowball fight,

Because nobody knows what's going to happen
The season's a sheet to scribble on
or a picture to paint, or some music to write
or a pitch for Clint to dribble on …

The season's stretched out like a beach
where we can run and play
and we feel that nothing's out of reach:
We'll be Champions come May!

Because

This is the beginning of the greatest season
this is the start of the ride
fasten your seat belts, take the brakes off …
See you at the other side!

First Match Breakfast

As I chew my toast and jam
I plot the thrashing of West Ham!

As I eat my bacon and eggs
I hope no Barnsley players break their legs!

As I chew my jam and toast
I plot their shots bouncing off our post!

As I eat my eggs and bacon
I know that I'll not be mistaken

When I wish Barnsley years in the very top flight
As sure as I take my coffee white!

9 August 1997
Barnsley 1 West Ham 2

The first game in the season, the most important game in Barnsley's history, and I missed it. I was on my holidays in Suffolk, about as far away from Barnsley as you could get. We were staying in a cottage and when I picked the key up I tried to engage the bloke in conversation. 'Big match today, then' I said. 'I don't follow football, I'm a speedway man myself' he said, and I felt a long long way from home.

We listened to the match in the red hot cottage; the kids put their Barnsley shirts on and I went to the toilet every time there was a free kick or a penalty, just like I do at Oakwell. When Redfearn scored I knew that all my dreams would come true, that Barnsley would stay in the premiership and that we'd get a place in Europe. It didn't really matter that we lost; we'd played well and Neil had scored. That night we watched *Match of the Day* and I blubbed.

12 August
Crystal Palace 0 Barnsley 1

Still on holiday and I could hardly get the radio to work; I had to stand there in the cottage like the Statue of Liberty, waving the radio round to get a bit of clear reception on Five Live. Another Redfearn goal: soon be time for the new lads to start scoring.

24 August
Barnsley 0 Chelsea 6

God, I was excited before this one, but not half as excited as my kids. My oldest was sick all over the place with sheer joy (well, that's what she told us). Went to Barnsley on the bus and couldn't believe the atmosphere; the band was playing, the crowd were singing and everything was right with the world. Just before the game a man behind me said 'Does tha know, I think it'll be nil-nil', and I believed him. Until the first goal went in. And then the second, and the third, and so on. You know the rest. The Chelsea fans started singing the song that we'd be singing back to so many teams that season, to the tune of *Knees Up Mother Brown*: 'You're not very good/You're not very good/You're not very /You're not very/You're not very good'. And we weren't really. But we were still optimistic: it would only be a minor blip. Barnard nearly scored.

Nil-Nil

Before the match
the man behind me said
'It'll be nil-nil'
and I nodded my head
and I thought
Nil-nil,
not bad,
fair result.

Then they scored a goal
and I said one-nil
and I started to feel
slightly ill

then they scored another
and I said two-nil
and Chelsea were showing
depressing skill

then they scored another
and I said three-nil
and I felt we were climbing
a Chelsea hill

then they scored another
and I said four-nil
and I felt like we were swallowing
a Chelsea pill

then they scored another
and I said five-nil
and Chelsea were putting us
through the mill

Then they scored another
and I said six-nil
and it felt like they were scoring
almost at will;

Still, there's always Bolton on Monday
Because Barnsley optimism is difficult to kill!

27 August
Barnsley 2 Bolton 1

After the Chelsea game Sky Sports rang me up: could I do a poem looking back at the Chelsea game and then one about the Bolton game? Could they record it at Oakwell? Of course I said yes (I always say yes) but then I began to get nervous. It's one thing recording a poem in your back garden but it's another thing recording one in front of the crowd at Oakwell. They wanted me to record the Chelsea poem before the match, do an instant poem at half time and then record a poem about the Bolton match the next day. So I stood on the edge of the pitch and did the poem, and people pointed at me and the director tried to get my embarrassed kids to join in, and then the match started and what an amazing match it was; Eric Tinkler and Gorgi Hristov scoring, David Watson getting stretchered off, Lars Leese coming back on to do an heroic job, and three more points in the bag. The next day I met the Sky Sports blokes and we filmed on a vantage point in Kendray where you could see the whole of Barnsley laid out in front of you. I still felt fantastically optimistic about the season; I knew we'd be okay.

30 August
Derby 1 Barnsley 0

The first away match we'd been able to get to, off to Derby's new ground at Pride Park, setting off really early on the supporters' coaches, getting to the ground about half past one, sitting in our seats watching the ground fill up. Having a good laugh at their mascot, Ronnie the Ram, who looked like a bloke with a ram's head and furry wellies on. We were sat very near the Derby fans and there was some excellent banter. At one point all the Barnsley fans, reliving old rivalries, sang 'I'd rather be a picket than a scab' to ironic applause from the Derby fans, apart from one old bloke who got really cross and stood up and shouted 'I am a Derbyshire miner and I was on strike for the whole year and proud of it!' to which the Barnsley fans replied 'Shut up and sit down, you daft old bugger'. Clint Marcelle got a goal early on that was disallowed, but we felt that we were going to win the game. Then Derby got a penalty. I didn't look, because I never look when we get penalties against us. I could tell by the cheers that Lars had saved it, but then the referee offered it to be taken again, and they got it that time. I didn't know it then, but we'd soon be cheering Ashley Ward.

13 September
Barnsley 0 Aston Villa 3

I found this game really depressing, because it felt like we were never going to win again. We shouted 'Miss! Miss!' at Gareth Southgate, but they still won us by three goals. I was due to go to Mexico filming in a couple of weeks, and I wanted us to win again before I went, or else I thought my plane might crash or something.

16 September - Coca-Cola Cup Second Round, First Leg
Chesterfield 1 Barnsley 2

I couldn't get to this one so me and the kids listened to it on the radio. If there's one thing worse than listening to the game on the radio, it's watching it on the ceefax, as the poem says. The worst thing is when you listen to it on the ceefax with your scarves and hat on, and have a pie at half time. Now that's really sad.

Ceefaxanorax

I'm a mad
sat in front of the Ceefax
sad sack anorak
That's me!

I'm a sad
staring at the motionless Ceefax
stone mad
anorak
That's me!

Come on you numbers, change
come on you Barnsley score
Come on letters rearrange
come on let's have one more

I'm a daft
squatting before the Ceefax
all adrift
Anorak
That's me!
I'm adrift
floating before the Ceefax
half daft
Anorak
That's me!

Come on you Ceefax watchers!
Come on you number crunchers
Come on you slumped on the settee
after too many liquid lunches!

We're all mad
Worshipping the Ceefax
Half daft
so sad
adrift
waiting for the score to change
Ceefaxanorax Ceefaxanorax Ceefaxanorax!

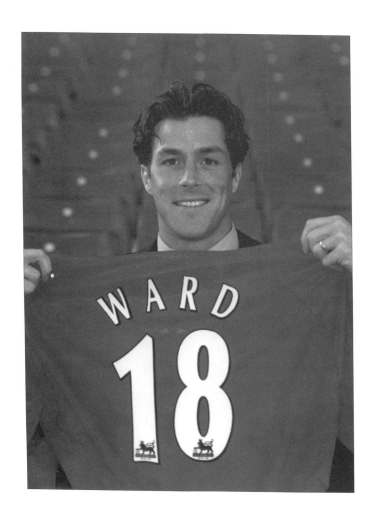

20 September
Everton 4 Barnsley 2

Just before we set off to this one the club rang up and asked if I'd be a steward on the bus. I said yes, but I was scared stiff. I've been on live telly and I've stood up in public in front of thousands of people but this was a daunting prospect. The selling of the scratchcards was the worst: keeping the change right, checking the winners, giving out more cards. Then I had to direct the driver with a little photocopied route sheet. I was relieved when we all got off the bus, but then as we got into the ground my lad was stung by a wasp. It proved to be a bad omen, as we lost four-two. Sitting on the coach on the way back, waiting to set off, Everton fans walked past holding up four and two fingers. Even when we did set off they were standing in their gardens holding up four and two fingers. Even when we'd left Liverpool there were people standing on bridges over the motorway holding up four and two fingers. We got back and I handed the money and the unused scratchcards in. They haven't asked me again, but I think I got the change right.

23 September
Wimbledon 4 Barnsley 1

I was packing for Mexico and listening to this on the radio and watching it on the ceefax at the same time. It didn't make any difference.

27 September
Barnsley 0 Leicester 2
30 September Coca Cola Cup Second Round, Second Leg
Barnsley 4 Chesterfield 1
4 October
Arsenal 5 Barnsley 0

I was filming in Mexico for all these games, and I can tell you that being a long way away from your team is much worse than listening to the game on the radio or watching it on the ceefax. I was staying in a hotel in Mexico City called the Hotel Bristol and telephone calls from the room were terrifyingly expensive. I would ring, say 'It's me' very quickly and my wife or one of my kids would say the score. And it cost me forty quid. Still, my plane didn't crash.

14 October - Coca Cola Cup, Third Round
Southampton 2 Barnsley 1

I was going to go in my Mexican hat to this one but at the last minute I chickened out. Things that look good when you're wearing them in Oaxaca look a bit daft on the X19 bus. It was freezing cold and we lost but it was great to be back, and I actually heard a bloke behind me say, as we crushed towards the exits 'Oh well, we can concentrate on the league now' and I never really thought anybody said that.

20 October
Barnsley 2 Coventry 0

There was still the problem of winning, though, and we solved the problem decisively at this game with goals from Redfearn and Ward. At the end we were so euphoric that we were singing 'Are you watching Manchester?' and we meant it and all!

People

People are writing us off,
people are starting to scoff,
people say that we're going down,
well whisper that in this beautiful town;

just because we're at the bottom of the table
doesn't mean that we're not able
to rise like a phoenix from the ashes,
fuelled by Andy Liddell's inspirational dashes!

People are writing us off,
people are starting to scoff;
people say we're heading for relegation,
well whisper that in Barnsley Bus Station!

I predict that we'll score three
against the Sky Blue Coventry,
anyway their manager, Gordon Strachan,
has hair like a clump of moorland bracken,
not like Danny Wilson's careful coiffure,
yes we're cut out for the Premiership for sure!

25 October
Manchester United 7 Barnsley 0

The Big One. I kept saying it to my kids. We'd say it to each other. The Big One. The Big One. I said it to fellow supporters I saw in town. We'd look determined and say The Big One. I had to do a poem for Radio Five Live. Ian Payne, the reporter, asked me after I'd recorded it, what I really thought we'd do. 'We'll win. It's The Big One' I said. He said that he thought it was a good time to be playing Manchester United and that he thought we'd probably get a draw. The Big One. I couldn't get a ticket so I sat in the back room with my kids and we heard the whole sorry humiliation. The Big One. The Big One.

Barnsley as Musical Centre of the Universe

The more they scored
The more we sang
And round Old Trafford
music rang.

The more they scored
The more we chanted
as Poborsky puffed
and Giggsy panted

Sing when you're winning?
Not today!
We sing when we're alive
That's the Barnsley way!

1 November
Barnsley 1 Blackburn Rovers 1

The best part of this match was singing 'Where's Your Shearer Gone' to the assembled pack of freezing cold Lancashiremen who, instead of a band, had a fat chap with a single drum. Every so often he'd bang it like somebody knocking on a door. They also sang their silly 'Lancashire TraLaLa/Lancashire TraLaLa' song, which made me laugh a lot.

8 November
Southampton 4 Barnsley 1

I think this was the low point of my season. I listened to it on the radio. I sat and looked at the walls. The kids couldn't bear to listen anymore. My wife went out of the room. I sat there on my own. The radio kept going off the station and I'd have to stand there holding it up just like I did for the Crystal Palace game all those months ago when the weather was boiling and the season was full of promise, but now instead of feeling like the Statue of Liberty I felt like a fat plonker with a radio in his hand.

Every Season

Every season something happens
to make you chuck the form book away;
well, I think summat's going to happen
at Anfield on Saturday!

Every season something happens
to put the smile back on your face
and I think summat's gunner happen
at Liverpool FC's place!

Every season something slips:
let it be the smile
from the Liverpool lips!

Every season something slides,
let it be Liverpool
when we tan their backsides!

Every season something happens
to prove football's still romantic
and I think summat's gunner happen
to drive Liverpool FC frantic!

22 November
Liverpool 0 Barnsley 1

If Southampton was the low point, this was the high point. On the Tuesday after the game, Sky Sports rang up and asked me if I could interview Ashley Ward that day. The problem was that I only had an hour gap, so I couldn't. They had another idea. They'd interview Ashley and then I could write a poem and they could film a dream sequence with me in bed dreaming about him scoring the goal, then waking up and thinking it was all a dream, and then going downstairs, turning on the telly and finding that it wasn't a dream after all. I said yes, knowing that my wife would be out at her mother's with the kids for that hour, because she's (understandably) not keen on the idea of people filming in the house. She went to her mother's and the Sky Sports people came. The cameraman asked for a bit of cardboard. I gave him some and he cut a window shape out of it and stuck a blue light behind it so that while I was lying in bed it looked like a deep blue moon was coming in through the window. It was quite difficult to film, and the cameraman had to lean right over me in bed, while the reporter had to lie next to me and fiddle with the lights. In the middle of filming my wife came home early. She found me lying in bed, bathed in artificial moonlight, next to a man in a suit, with a man and a camera straddling me. I can explain, I said. I think I sounded convincing.

Barnsley One, Liverpool Nil

Ward scored
on an Autumn day
and all our troubles
slipped away!

Ward scored
in the Liverpool net
and this game was
the greatest yet!

They thought they were better
but we were the best,
now just bring on
all the rest!

They thought we were weak
but we were strong
now let the others
roll along!

Ward scored
and the dream was back on track
thanks to Wardy's goal
we're never looking back!

Wardy scored!
Wardy scored!
Wardy scored!

(Repeat until exhausted…)

Praise Poem for Arjan de Zeeuw

Arjan de Zeeuw!
Arjan de Zeeuw!
Let me sing
what I know is true!

Arjan de Zeeuw!
Arjan de Zeeuw!
our defensive wall
is built round you!

Arjan de Zeeuw!
Arjan de Zeeuw!
You helped pull off
our Anfield coup!

The Barnsley Dutchman
with flat cap and clogs
every morning I see you
walking your dogs;
and I fall down on my knees
and I shout 'Arjan!
You're my favourite
Dutchman!'

Arjan de Zeeuw!
Arjan de Zeeuw!
Let me sing
what I know is true!

29 November
Barnsley 2 Leeds United 3

God, it was cold. And wet. I looked at my programme from this match the other day and all the pages were stuck together with sogginess. And this was the start of us losing games to late goals.

In Defence of Barnsley Women

Poor old Gorgi Hristov got pilloried for apparently saying that Barnsley women were ugly. He didn't say it, but I wrote a poem for the girls I grew up with.

I swear by the holes in my string vest
That Barnsley women are the best!

From Market Hill to Eldon Street
They're the nicest women you could meet,

and it seems a shame that, once again,
The Press with its funny Southern brain

has put the spotlight on our town
made us out to be the nation's clown

full of ugly sisters and warty hags
clutching tripe-filled shopping bags.

Well, let me tell you what I know is true
as my heart is red and the sky is blue

that the women of Barnsley beat the lot
for brains and beauty, and I'm not

the sort of bloke to stand and leer
at women clutching pints of beer;

these are the Nineties, women can be
anything they want, you see,

tall or short, fat or thin,
quiet, or making an enormous din

so let's all shout it, let's not rest
from saying Barnsley Women are the Best!

Raise the banners, shout it loud,
Barnsley Women make us proud!

And let's hope that soon the London press
will use another doorstep to drop their mess!

6 December
Sheffield Wednesday 2 Barnsley 1

This was the one where DiCanio, who should have been sent off by our mate Mr Willard, was still on the pitch and scored just before the end of the match. The day after, I was giving out some prizes at a school in Doncaster. The deputy head, announcing me, said 'We'd like to show Mr McMillan what a difference a minute can make in someone's life'. I nodded, uncomprehending. They got a big video screen out. 'Don't you agree that a minute can make a big difference in someone's life?' he said. Yes, I said. Then they switched the video on and showed the bloody DiCanio goal. Three times!

13 December
Barnsley 2 Newcastle United 2

Afterwards I was talking to some Newcastle fans who were bitterly disappointed in their team, and I wondered, as I often do, what makes us put ourselves through this pain and torture every week. I tend to agree with Frank Skinner when he says that he's been as happy as he's ever likely to be and as unhappy as he's ever likely to be when he's watching football, and although it's not an answer, it's a reason.

How To Beat Spurs

We must be tighter at the back
than my Grandma's corset,
We must be sharper at the front
than my Grandma's bra
We must be quick on the turn
like a well-greased faucet
and zoom with the speed
of a well-oiled car!

We must get the ball like Uncle Charlie
used to get the ball off me
when we played Subbuteo
after Sunday tea!

We must have more defence
than my Grandad's toolshed
We must have more attack
than my Grandad's dog,
We must have some belief
in the poem we've just read
then beating Spurs will be easier
than falling off a log!

20 December
Spurs 3 Barnsley 0

Another sad afternoon in the back room trying to tune the radio in. People said we'd be relegated by Christmas, though, and we weren't, so there was still something to cheer about.

In Defence of Middlesbrough and Barnsley

The Evening Standard wrote about foreign footballers enjoying the South more than the North, so I had to write a poem very quickly.

Here come those fools
from the South again
saying our towns are dreadful!
Well let me tell you
it's a pain
and I've had a headful!

Middlesbrough and Barnsley
are lovely places
full of decent folk;
you've only to look
at our happy smiles
to know we're not a joke!

Look again you fool
from the deepest South
our towns shine like well-brushed teeth;
we think you ought to
shut your mouth
I mean, have you seen Bexleyheath?

26 December
Bolton 1 Barnsley 1
Holding the radio up. Alcoholic haze. Wearing my new Barnsley hat and my Homer Simpson socks.

28 December
Barnsley 1 Derby 0
This was the start of the revival; this was the start of the time when we really did feel that we could stay up. It was a cold day and Wardy scored a red hot goal. Yorkshire Television rang up wanting me to do a series for the Tonight Programme about the club. I wasn't sure. Still, it might be a laugh.

3 January
Barnsley 1 Bolton 0 - FA Cup Third Round
The revival continues. Survival possible or probable.

10 January
West Ham 6 Barnsley 0
By this time I was well into writing my weekly poem for the Barnsley Chronicle, and people often commented on it when they saw me at the match. I like the idea of a poet being a public figure, rather than somebody scribbling in a room. I would write the poems on a Wednesday morning, making sure they were the right length to fit the space I was allocated at the bottom of the letters page. This was a depressing match but I was sure it was only a blip in our continued upward progress. A man from German Television rang up and said he'd like to film me at some point.

Double Trouble

We beat 'em once
We can beat 'em again
In the wind, or the fog
or the pouring rain!

We beat 'em in the Summer
when the sun was hot
Now we'll beat 'em in the Winter
when it's really not!

Redfearn got the goal
that sent 'em on their way,
I think he'll do it again
this Saturday!

What have they got?
A bald Italian!
What have we got?
A Macedonian Stallion!

We beat 'em once
now for the double
Crystal Palace
have got Double Trouble!

Because we beat 'em once
We can beat 'em twice
and if Spurs also lose
that would be really nice!

17 January
Barnsley 1 Crystal Palace 0

A man shook my hand at the match. 'Lucky handshake' he said. 'As long as I keep shaking your hand we won't lose'. I felt a great sense of responsibility. Still, we won this one.

24 January - FA Cup Fourth Round
Spurs 1 Barnsley 1
31 January
Chelsea 2 Barnsley 0

Two more afternoons trying to tune the radio in. Why isn't the Chelsea match on the end of season video?

4 February - FA Cup Fourth Round Replay
Barnsley 3 Spurs 1

During the match I shouted to Ginola 'My wife thinks you're the most handsome man who ever lived', but I don't think he heard me. It was a wonderful game and I began to feel optimistic again. Spring and survival weren't too far away. The man from German Television said he'd like to come and film me at the Everton game. The man from Yorkshire Television said that he'd like to come and film me at the Everton game. A woman from ABC News of America said she'd like to film me at the Everton game but I put her off by saying that there would be two other film crews there and she said 'Well, Ian, I like to be there when there are no other crews around.'

7 February
Barnsley 2 Everton 2

The night before, the man from German TV rang and said that his plane had been cancelled so he'd be arriving the next morning. 'I land in Manchester at ten to twelve, so I should be with you at half past' he said. 'I don't think you will' I said. He eventually arrived at ten past two. I was being filmed by Yorkshire TV so he filmed me being filmed by Yorkshire. I sat in my seat and every time I did anything two cameras filmed it. It was an odd experience; a bit like being on holiday with relatives who wouldn't stop videoing you.

Watson, D

Watson, D
listen to me
don't let them have
a scoring spree!
Your learning curve
in the premiership
has been as twisted
as an Elvis lip!
So Watson, D,
Listen to me
don't let them have
a scoring spree!

15 February - FA Cup Fifth Round
Manchester United 1 Barnsley 1

I'd got tickets for me and the kids for this game, but the bloke from Yorkshire Television wanted to film me going to the match with the Ora Band, so my wife had to go to that match. Afterward she said she couldn't see what all the fuss was about. I had to film with the band in a club in the middle of Manchester that was full of equal numbers of Barnsley fans and Manchester United fans. The atmosphere was raucous but friendly, although someone from the band said to me, as a fan hit himself on the head with a beer tray in tune to the music 'If we get out of here alive I'll stand for't egg under't cap'. I knew what he meant. After we'd filmed in the club I had to lead the band through the streets of Manchester to Old Trafford, being filmed as we walked. United fans chucked chips at us, but it was all in good fun. We hadn't managed to get a press pass for the game so I had to listen to one of the greatest matches in Barnsley's history in the TV producer's car parked a hundred yards from the ground.

Justice

A cry rang across the entire town
When Neville brought our Liddell down

And we all shouted 'Referee
It's got to be a penalty!'

But the silly man just waved Play On
and our winning chance seemed to be gone

and of course we drew at Man United
and of course we should be so delighted

and of course we'll win 'em here next week
and of course their cup prospects are bleak

but it leaves a bitter, bitter taste
when a ref lets a penalty go to waste.

21 February
Coventry 1 Barnsley 0

I think I'm getting old, but all the way to Coventry I was busting for a wee. I managed to last until we got to the ground then I had to give my hat and scarf to a bloke I knew and run like hell to a vast pub full of Coventry fans.

Dive Time

Put it up in lights
of the brightest neon:
we were done down
by Diving Dion!

We watched a game
that wasn't a classic
but the referee
was quite jurassic!

And as we walked
back to the bus
fans said 'Will you write
this poem for us?'

But the words they said
a family paper can't use,
let's just say that we had
the Sky Blue blues!

25 February - FA Cup Fifth Round Replay
Barnsley 3 Manchester United 2

One of the greatest nights ever. One of those nights that sport sometimes hands you when everything seems possible.

28 February
Barnsley 2 Wimbledon 1

The woman from ABC News of America wanted to film me and the bloke from Yorkshire TV wanted to film me and I did what I often do which is say yes to both of them and hope that something will turn up. The woman from ABC News had said 'Don't forget. No other crews' so I was a bit nervous. I had to go down to Sleaford with Yorkshire Television first to film Malcolm Moyes and his fanzine, then zoom up with Malcolm to some filming in the Outpost pub, then run to the car park at the ground to be filmed by ABC news then I had to go to another part of the car park to do a bit more with YTV. It almost worked, except I forgot to take my YTV microphone off when I ran down to the car park to be filmed by ABC. The woman from ABC was very cross and although they filmed me I don't think they ever showed it. Oh well, we won.

Let's Have 'Em

Manchester beaten
Wimbledon beaten
now I'm looking forward to
Sunday's meetin'

Up the A1
in bus or car
to Why Aye land
where the Geordies are

one more step
to the FA Cup
and the only way
from here is up!

Two more games
then a Wembley trip
to wipe the sneer
from the cynic's lip,

Manchester flattened,
Wimbledon same
Now I can't wait for
Sunday's game!

8 March - FA Cup Quarter-Final
Newcastle 3 Barnsley 1

I went to my mate Stuart McHale's with the kids to watch it on his telly. I took a bottle of champagne for when we won. I put it in his fridge. We lost. I took it out of his fridge and took it home. Concentrate on the league, then.

11 March
Aston Villa 0 Barnsley 1

This was difficult because I was giving a talk at Swinton Library while the match was on. I told the audience that at half time in the match I'd ring home on the mobile phone and see how we were getting on, and if we were winning then the whole audience had to cheer. I rang and my daughter answered; all the audience were at the edge of their seats. 'We're winning one nil' she said. I told the audience and you could hear the cheers as far as Mexbrough.

14 March
Barnsley 4 Southampton 3

I often miss goals because I'm so nervous I have to go to the toilet. I confess that when I get down to the toilet I often don't go. I just stand there for a minute and then come back. There were loads of goals in this game and I missed two. To the people who sit around me it was a big joke, but I really couldn't help it. I resolved to try and stay at least forty-five minutes next week.

Southampton Chewed Up

They came all the way
from the far south coast
and we had 'em just like
beans on toast!

They'd beaten us twice,
thought they'd make it three
but we swallowed 'em like
a cup of tea!

When we emerged
the 4-3 winners
it was like we'd had
the best of dinners!

And now what would be better
than a cheesy dip
would be if we stayed
in the Premiership!

The Time is Now

I start getting itchy
on a Thursday
I start getting twitchy
on a Friday,

on Saturday morning
I can hardly speak
as we approach the climax
of the week,

get the bus to the ground
join the throng
in a stirring, swelling
Barnsley song;

it's nearly three o'clock
the hour is coming,
hear the ORA Band's
frantic drumming,

then as Owen puts Germoline
on his spots
Watson keeps out Liverpool's
feeble shots!

28 March
Barnsley 2 Liverpool 3

I couldn't believe the referee in this match and I couldn't believe my own reactions. I turned from a mild-mannered family man to a heap of snarling rage. I felt helpless and impotent and afterwards I did the sort of thing chaps like me do: I wrote letters, one to the football club expressing my support, one to David Mellor and one to the FA. I don't know how much good it did but it made me feel better to bash the computer keys. I suspect that for many people the season ended here.

Man in the Middle

It seems to me
that a referee
holds the game
in the palm of his hand,

and when he walked away
last Saturday
I stood in horror
in the Lower East Stand;

his three red cards
were far too hard
why he did it
I couldn't understand,

and my blame
for that awful game
goes to the man
with the whistle
in his hand …

31 March
Blackburn Rovers 2 Barnsley 1

The only good thing about this match was that I'd found a good position for the radio so that I could hear it properly. Maybe next season I'll get a new radio.

4 April
Leeds United 2 Barnsley 1

I guess this match will be remembered for Adie's own goal but I want to remember it for the Leeds fans who told me that they hoped we'd stay up, for Gorgi's goal and for the banner the lads in front of me held up that said 'Free Deirdre, Jail Willard'. There's a bit of cultural history!

Cheer Up

Cheer up, Adie
It's not your fault,
settle back and have
a single malt

(Well, maybe two)

Cheer up Gorgi
and button your lip
swearing's not allowed
in the Premiership

(ask Paul Ince!)

Cheer up Danny
Life is hard
Give the team
A good luck card

(Not a red one!)

Cheer up Barnsley
there's still time
In May I'll be writing
my survival rhyme

(I'm sure I will!)

11 April
Barnsley 2 Sheffield Wednesday 1

This was a joyous win. The Wednesday fans sang 'Danny's Coming Home' and we shouted 'No Way!' Near where I sit, Johnny Hendrie tackled DiCanio and tore his sock. DiCanio started shouting and the Wednesday Physio ran on; we wondered why, because nobody seemed to be injured but then he put his hand over DiCanio's mouth to stop him shouting. The Wednesday band played the Great Escape about ten million times but it didn't do them any good.

13 April
Newcastle United 2 Barnsley 1

The old problem again. I was dying for a wee before we got on the M1 and as we approached Scotch Corner services I went to the steward on the bus and told him a lie. I said that I'd had a bladder operation the week before and I wasn't fully recovered. I could tell he didn't believe me and I had to hang on until the Washington services, when I ran across the bridge like Quasimodo. The old problem again: a late goal. Still, at least Jan Aage wasn't badly injured.

A1 Thoughts

As we were herded back
to our away fans' bus
the geordies all made
fun of us

striped like zebras
they all sneered
and waved their fists
and crowed and jeered

but we'd seen them
sitting stunned
as their millionnaires
were outgunned

by the men in red
who nearly won
and as the buses drove
through the setting sun

I thought of the game
on Saturday
when we'll show the reds
just how to play!

Barnsley Two Spurs Nil

I reckon
Division One beckons
for Spurs on Saturday!

I think it's true
the Barnsley Crew
will blow the Spurs away!

For far too long
people have said
some teams are too big to go down
I think they're wrong
get it into your head
we're survivors in this Northern town!

I swear
by Ginola's hair
that Spurs will wash and go!

I estimate
by Gross's pate
we will win – two zero!

For far too long
people have said
Barnsley are for the chop;
I think they're wrong
get it into your head
that Spurs are for the drop!

18 April
Barnsley 1 Spurs 1

The big one. The big one. Everybody I met in town said it. The big one. For some reason we all shook hands, everybody around me shaking hands with each other before the start of the game. The big one. The big one. And a draw wasn't really enough. We saw Gross's pate gleaming in the sun. I didn't go to the toilet all the way through the match. Maybe I knew that the season was slipping away.

Numbers Game

Nine points left,
Nine precious points
to keep us
at the top!

Nine points left
Nine golden points
to save us
from the drop!

We could pick up three,
gather six
or even
win the lot

then next year
we'll be there
to get that Europe spot!

25 April
Barnsley 0 Arsenal 2

The big one. We said it again. 'They're due to lose' said a man near me in the pie queue, 'and it could be this one they lose'. Of course, they won, and people round me started singing 'Champions, champions' at the Arsenal fans. They clapped us, which riled a man near me. 'Ah, yer wouldn't be clapping us if we'd won yer!' he yelled. Which is true.

Three Little Words

Not down yet!
Not down yet!
Shout it till
Your tonsils sweat!

Not yet down!
Not yet down!
Sing it all
around the town!

Down yet? Not!
Down yet? Not!
Give it everything
You've got!

Three little words
said with pride
to keep us from
the Nationwide!

2 May
Leicester City 1 Barnsley 0

I couldn't even get to a radio for this one, because I was rehearsing for a show. I had to rely on somebody else's radio. He came up to me after a while, and the look on his face said it all. 'I've got some bad news for you, mate' he said. The dream was over.

We'll Be Back!

So we've fallen
down the hole
put there by
a Leicester goal!

So we've fallen
through the floor
but we'll be back
through the trapdoor!

So we're down
but we're not done
and we'll climb back
to the sun!

One ray of light
makes life still pretty
at least we're not fans of
Manchester City!

10 May
Manchester United 2 Barnsley 0

I was filming again for Yorkshire TV for this one, and I think we all wanted it to be something special, but it felt a bit subdued. The crowd were tired, the players were tired. The rain came down and the season ran away in a splash of muddy water. Our spirits were lifted at the end, though, when Toby Tyke did a Full Monty for us all. Back at home I drank my champagne but my heart wasn't in it. Still, we'll be back. We'll be back.

Quick Returns

We sang
'You'll never
walk alone'

We crowned
King Danny
On his throne

In the pouring
rain
some stood alone

Thinking how
our team
had grown

and how
our Premier time
had flown

but we'll be back
cos we're just
on loan

To Division One, that is!----

Just Like Watching Brazil

A script written for a Radio Four production. A poem for the whole season.

Crowd: It's just like watching Brazil, it's just like watching Brazil, it's just like watching Brazil.
Commentator: We are in for a treat this afternoon, the early eight minutes, we've seen some nice football.
Crowd: There's only one Danny Wilson, one Danny Wilson, walking along, singing our song, walking in a winter wonderland.
Boy: We go in the door and it just feels like a new world. There's all the fans singing. There's a load of big kids who start all the songs off and they've invited us up for the match.

IAN

Welcome to the carnival, welcome to a place
Built on sweat at a black coal face
Welcome to the carnival, welcome to a town
Where the pit wheel spun and the cage fell down.
Welcome to the carnival, welcome to the dream
Kept on the boil by a winning team

OLD MAN

Been watching 'em for years. On the Ponty End
Used to shout 'Gerrim in't wall bottom! Send
Him straight to't coal face.' You could, then
Seemed like a game of men against men

Now you have to sit down, and if you stand up
You get told to sit down by some jumped up
Steward who thinks he's God's youngest lad
And doesn't know I worked next to his dad.
For thirty years on the Silkstone seam
And played beside him in the Welfare team.
Sit down! We've been sitting down too long!
And you have to stand up

if you want to sing your song
Wife'll think I'm daft, but who cares…

IAN
Brazil, it's just like watching Brazil
It's just like watching Brazil
It's just like watching Brazil…

CHORUS
Football looks back to the glory that's been
And on to the glory to come
But the moment of the game
Is a dazzling thing
Like staring too long at the sun
Like staring too long at the sun.

GIRL
Got my balloons
Got my flag
And I'm ready to sing
And I love this moment more than anything.
Not much round here to stay for
My mates all said
The jobs are gone
And the town's half dead.
Well they should be here
When the crowd starts to move
In a town that's got
So much to prove…

IAN
This is where the excitement grows
Shouts in your ears and smells in your nose

Fans: Steak and kidney pie please. Half-time draw, pound a go. Roll up, roll up.
Spray can rattles. Are you having your face done? Yes. What do you want
written on it? Same as that love.

IAN

Welcome to the carnival, come and join the throng
History is the singing, winning is the song!
The carnival that's football
A slice of Barnsley heaven
And heaven came to Barnsley
in 1997…

Commentator: It's Marcelle in the penalty area, can he seal it here for Barnsley?
Yes he can, the man from the Caribbean brings Premiership football to South
Yorkshire with a wonderful goal. Barnsley are heading to Utopia…

IAN

What a moment for a town
That's always been a joke
See the grown men weep
Hear the voices choke

Commentator: Oakwell is alive, it's all red and white.

OLD MAN

When Kennedy was shot I was down the pit
When Elvis died I was down the pit
When they sunk the Belgrano I was down the pit
When the hurricane struck the south I was down the pit

When they landed on the moon
I didn't really care
But when Barnsley beat Bradford
I was there…

Commentator: The referee has taken a signal from both his linesmen, and that's
it, after ninety-nine years in the football league, unfashionable Barnsley are up, up
and away. Next season they will rub shoulders with the Premiership millionaires.

IAN

After the full time whistle went
I looked around the stands
And some were cheering and crying
And some were clapping their hands
And some were standing, just standing still
Feeding on the moment, drinking their fill
I could see them looking in the champagne air
For the mates who'd died, and should have been there
For the parents who took them and stood in the cold
For year after year, who just wouldn't be told
That Barnsley would never have a place in the sun
It's for people like that that this game was won.

Commentator: And I think the man who has the sun shining on him at the moment more than anybody else is Danny Wilson who is along side me. Many many congratulations.

Danny: Thank you, thank you, yes, great. Fantastic achievement. If you look at faces down there, there is a lot of old men very emotional and there is an old man here very emotional as well. These lot fully deserve it, they've been tremendous this season.

Commentator: Has it done something for the community at large? Is it more than football or not?

Danny: It's much more than football without a doubt. They've had hard times down here for the last decade or so, and this is the type of relief that they've been needing.

CHORUS

Football looks back to the glory that's been
And on to the glory to come
But the moment of the game
Is a dazzling thing
Like staring too long at the sun
Like staring too long at the sun.

Sprinkler sprays water on the pitch at Oakwell

GIRL
I love that time just before the new season, but this one was even more special.

Voice: Don't walk on that pitch

IAN
With the new signings, blinking at press conferences in their suits.

OLD MAN
Photo's in the Barnsley Chronicle

GIRL
Pre season friendlies

IAN
Expanding the ground; new car park

OLD MAN
And the money flowing into the club

GIRL
Money like we'd never seen before.

IAN
Money pouring from a golden pot

OLD MAN
Media money seeping across the floor

Fan: For a while now, Barnsley have been slammed in the media, it is right back to the flat caps and whippet syndrome. The one thing that Premiership football did was to pull the community of Barnsley together, and the media joined in with us then. After being absent during the dark and desperate days, they were almost out of control in Barnsley trying to find the celebratory stories.

IAN

And now the spotlight was on the town
And the circus came to view our carnival
And the pack were parked outside the ground
Like support bands at a festival…

GIRL

Exciting times, with the BBC
And Sky and newspapers and ITV
Making us out to be the kind of place
That deserves the camera in its face

Dave Beresford: I think what we'd like to do is talk to him outside on the pitch.

OLD MAN

I saw the cameras, and thought of '84
Cos that's when the telly was here before
When the strike was on and the headline news
Was a riot shield or a picket's bruise

Dave Beresford: Hi Danny, Dave Beresford.
Danny: Hi Dave, where do you want to do it?
Dave Beresford: Out on the pitch. We'll need to put a microphone on you.

IAN

Now the wires are there and the microphone's ready
And the lights are on and the camera's steady
And here's the distillation of false and true
The pre-match post-match interview

Danny: Shall I leave my jacket undone?
Dave Beresford: Yeah, or do it up. It's up to you. Whatever you are comfortable with.

GIRL

Danny Wilson always came across as honest

IAN
Straight questions, straight answers.

OLD MAN
Some of 'em never look you in the eye

GIRL
Strike you as villains, strike you as chancers.

OLD MAN
But Wilson always told you straight.

IAN
With his shoulder bearing a whole town's weight . . .

Media Crew: Right then chaps, bit of movement to get into it. Camera about there please.

IAN
When Danny is ready
The interview will start
A delicate, fending, probing art
When Danny is ready
The questions begin
But they all boil down to one

Media Crew: Alright then, Running. Speed. OK...

Will we, can we bloody Win?

CHORUS
Football looks back at the glory that's been
And on to the glory to come
But the moment of the game
Is a dazzling thing
Like staring too long at the sun
Like staring too long at the sun

IAN

The dressing room
The room where the players get ready for work room
Feel the pressure of the 18,000 fans outside
Feel the pressure of yourself inside
The dressing room
Clothes laid out ready, shirts, socks,
Shorts, pants. The game
Always the game
Always the game
The dressing room
The pressing room
The room where the jokes
Stick in your throat
Feel the pressure of the 18,000 fans inside
Feel the pressure of yourself outside
And always the game
And always the game
And nobody wants to sit on the subs bench
Nobody wants to fail
And the 'Away' players dressing rooms
The chicken hut … hot …
All those millions of pounds
Sitting in the chicken hut
Waiting, waiting
Spirits wilting
In the chicken hut
And the shower rooms.
Where you can wash away the memory
Of that missed opportunity
Scrub away the tension
Of that own goal
And the time is getting closer
and the time is getting nearer
and in the boot room
all those goals
all those free kicks

waiting, waiting, waiting
in pairs
for the afternoon to take them
unawares
and the time is getting closer
and the time is getting nearer

CHORUS
And the moment of the game
Is a dazzling thing
Like staring too long at the sun
Like staring too long at the sun

Crowd: Next year we'll be champions, next year we'll be champions

GIRL
Always get there early for the pre-match rush
And the noise and the shouting and the delicious crush
And the way that when you get round to five to three
You're floating on a singing, cheering sea…

IAN
And some of us are nervous
And some of us are mad

GIRL
And some of us are shouting
And some of us are bad

OLD MAN
And some of us are ancient

GIRL
and some of us are young

ALL
And we make the ritual noise
from the collective lung

Tannoy: Welcome to the house of fun, now I've come of age, welcome to the house of fun, temptation's on its way.

OLD MAN
Good to see the big crowds back; we've seen
Hard times here, gates so small
You looked round and you knew them all
And we're related to most of them
And at half time you walked to the other end
To stand behind the goals
And stamp your feet in the freezing rain
Though your socks were full of holes
And I never thought I'd see this day
I never thought I'd feel so good
And I can't wait to see the buggers play
This season's goona be good!

Crowd: Ee-aye, ee-aye, oh, top class football here we go.

IAN
And now the season starts
And 18,000 hearts
Are bursting with Barnsley Pride

GIRL
And the noise hits you
Like a football in the face
The minute you walk inside…

IAN
Three o'clock and the samba band
Are banging out a rhythm in the Ora Stand

OLD MAN
Your life's built for this, for the moment when
The fanfare begins and it all comes round again

IAN
You were born for this, beneath a Barnsley sky
and the Oakwell hopes will never die.

GIRL
On a white hot day in the Summer sun
The premier adventure is well and truly on

OLD MAN
Danny Wilson's army, proud and strong
Lifting up our voices in the Barnsley Song

Commentator: Corner's taken, left hand side, nobody has claimed it, West Ham haven't got it away yet...

Then the unthinkable happened and we took the lead
Oh, this was truly life, indeed!

Commentator: Header down and a header in, and a goal from Barnsley scored by their captain Redfearn and Barnsley have scored. Barnsley one, West Ham United nil and Neil Redfearn the captain has scored their very first goal in the big time.

CHORUS
Football looks back to the glory that's been
And on to the glory to come
But the moment of the game
Is a dazzling thing
Like staring too long at the sun
Like staring too long at the sun

Lazaridis has turned things round in the second half and Barnsley are slumping here, having had such a magnificent start to this game, they trail West Ham by two goals to one.

OLD MAN
But then we started to lose
Aye, and the defeats
Piled up like litter on deserted streets

Petrescu left footed, hits the post it goes in and that's a goal for Chelsea, it's Barnsley nil, Chelsea one. Oh, that's a great chance and he scores. Barnsley nil, Chelsea two. Chelsea three. Chelsea four. It's five-nil. Chelsea six.

GIRL
And everytime you turned on *Match of the Day*
You saw our defence being blown away.

IAN
Chelsea got six
Six hammer blows
That resonated down to my Barnsley toes

Commentator: Bergkamp right foot shot and Dennis Bergkamp scores an absolutely magnificent goal for Arsenal to put them ahead. Through to the edge of the penalty area and Dennis Bergkamp will make it two-nil. Three-nil to Arsenal. It's Arsenal four, Barnsley nil. Five-nil to Arsenal.

IAN
And as Summer turned to Winter
And the leaves began to fall
It felt like we would win...

OLD MAN
Sod All!

Boy: It's just that first season you've got to cope with, after that you'll be alright. Same with Leicester, they've done really well this season, it's just that first year. Danny: I think at the end of the day we deserve to be in the Premiership because we finished second in the league last year and I think that our lads have to believe in themselves like they did last year.
Fan: Every game is a celebration, even at three-nil, four-nil, five-nil. We were

shouting at four-nil, we were singing we were going to win five-four. At five-nil we were going to win six-five. And eventually we ended up just two minutes from time singing we're going to win seven-six.
Crowd: Danny Wilson's red and white army, Danny Wilson's red and white army, Danny Wilson's red and white army.

IAN
Danny Wilson's red and white army

OLD MAN
We love you Barnsley, we do

GIRL/IAN
And as we sang and as we danced

OLD MAN
We hoped the words were true!

Samba band play Ilkley Moor Baht Hat

IAN
But you've got to stand by your team
When things are going wrong
You've got to wave your flag
And sing your song
We didn't get this far not to sing and dance
This could be our one and only chance.

OLD MAN
What?

IAN
This could be our one and only time.

GIRL
This might be it.

IAN
One season wonders.

OLD MAN
This might be it.

GIRL
Straight back down

GIRL
This might be it

IAN
The whipping boys

OLD MAN
This might be it

IAN
We're a worthless, no hope cartoon town.

Bugle plays the Funeral March.

OLD MAN
Well, some said they never wanted it
Never wanted top flight football brushing it
It cost too much to get it
It cost too much to stay there
Carry on playing Rochdale,
Carry on playing Crewe
Remember top flight football
Is not for the likes of you

GIRL
You've got to remember that this isn't made up

OLD MAN
This isn't a story from out of a book

IAN
This is a slice of '90s real

OLD MAN
How football can make you truly feel

IAN
That you're part of something, of a wider stage,

GIRL
And the Premier's the volume

IAN
And Oakwell is the page

The sound of brush polishing boots, mixing to rain, wind, horses hooves.

OLD MAN
And the winter came
And the days grew colder
And I started off the season old
And now I'm four months older
I thought of that other Winter
When the pit wheels stopped turning
And there was nothing left to feed our kids
And only muck for burning
And defeat was everywhere around
And the coppers' horses made a frightening sound
And the Winter froze us solid
Didn't melt us back to work
But when the Spring began to thaw us
How our hearts and fingers hurt.

CHORUS
Like staring too hard at the sun
Like staring too hard at the sun

Commentator: Up to the edge of the penalty area, it's in towards Ward, Ward with a shot, ohhh and Ward has scored for Barnsley. Barnsley one, Coventry nil. Neil Redfearn runs forward and scores. Two-nil. He buries it into the top of the net.

OLD MAN
And the season picked up
And we picked up points
And I picked up the samba
And my aching joints
And Redfearn, Fjortoft, Ashley Ward
Picked up results by playing hard
And the days were cold but the football steamed
And my hands were frozen and my nostrils streamed
But I felt it didn't matter
As I sang the stupid songs
And it felt like we'd be staying up
Up where we belonged!

Commentator: Well there is total confusion here, that is all I can tell you. The game has been stopped, Chris Morgan is the second Barnsley player to be sent off after Darren Barnard. But the referee Gary Willard has left the pitch together with his two referee's assistants.

IAN
Liverpool three Barnsley two
Barnsley down to eight
And it felt to me that something stank
Something wasn't right
'We've only got nine men' we sang
So another got the card
And it felt like we were learning
But the lesson's bloody hard

Julian Wroe: The Liverpool game at home was the turning point in Barnsley's season, when we perhaps really did know what the term professional meant, in terms of professional football. Because there were some very professional activities going off there, that I think were part and parcel of ruining Barnsley's season.

IAN

This was the game when a lot of people's season
ended; when the Lord of Unreason
Ruled, and the beautiful game
Had a black eye and a bloody nose to its name

Julian Wroe: There were three players sent off, Barnsley were down to eight men and the very fact that Liverpool only won in the last two or three minutes by the odd goal said a lot for Barnsley's resilience, it said even more about the kind of tactics that the big professional clubs can resort to to win games.

IAN

This was the game where innocence went
where the face paints faded
And the singing died.
This was the game where a lot of fans
Lost the will to win inside

Boy: Morgan and Barnard got sent off for fouling Michael Owen and Sheridan got sent off for dissent. It weren't fair at all.
Fan: There's no gamesmanship in the Premiership. It's all prima donnas. It seems to be anyroad.

OLD MAN

And it felt like the premier was slipping away
As if the season was just one long long day
Now it was the evening, and the night was coming on
And the day was running out of time
the day would soon be gone

Crowd: Always look on the bright side of life

Commentator: Now then, a chance for Guppy on the left of the area, he's clear, across it comes, great save, and a chance and a goal for Zagorakis. Zagorakis taps it in to the empty net, Leicester take the lead and Barnsley now surely are back in Division One.

IAN
Defeat is never very good
Defeat is never pretty

OLD MAN
But we don't want your handkerchiefs
We don't want your pity

Commentator: And there is the final whistle and it's all over for Barnsley in the Premiership. You look at the red shirts and Neil Redfearn is shaking the hand of the referee. Nicky Eaden has got his hands on his knees, alone with his thoughts. You've got to feel for those Barnsley players, they're going to go to those Barnsley fans now, the team have done tremendously, the fans have done tremendously, but it's not been enough and here at Filbert Street in the Spring sunshine there's dark clouds over Barnsley.

Fan: The visit to Leicester was the game that Barnsley had to win. We didn't. The net result was the same as the net result of one year before, exactly to the day, when we'd beaten Bradford. There was still the same carnival atmosphere, there was still same songs, there was still the tears down the face and there was still a fair few minutes of silence.

Fans: It's still like watching Brazil, it's still like watching Brazil.

GIRL
We might be down to Division One
Our hopes and dreams might be dead and gone

IAN
But football's about next Saturday's game
When winning's the thing, and Barnsley's the name.

GIRL
And now we've tasted the Premier
Now we've been at the top, well

OLD MAN
We prefer Champagne
to old flat pop!

Crowd: On loan to the Nationwide, on loan to the Nationwide.

OLD MAN
This town has been dragged through the dust
Felt history's boot in its balls
As the pithead gear succumbs to rust
and the closed-down shaft roof falls.
And the season might fade here and now
But football never dies
And this town feels the future
Shining out of its eyes!

CHORUS
Football looks back to the glory that's been
And on to the glory to come
But the moment of the game
Is a dazzling thing
Like staring too long at the sun
Like staring too long at the sun

Crowd: Danny Wilson's red and white army, Danny Wilson's red and white army...

OLD MAN
I can't believe it

GIRL
Wilson's gone

OLD MAN
And I was sure he was going to carry on

GIRL
I don't want to believe it

OLD MAN
The king is dead

GIRL
And after all he's done and said

Danny: What I said before was that I had two years of my contract still to run and I fully expected to be there, but who knows what's round the corner. They'll understand, the fans at Barnsley are very, very fair. They're very open minded, they'll understand the situation far greater than a lot of people will give them credit for.

Fan: It's a shock.
Fan: Bit shocked, I didn't think he'd do it, but.
Fan: There was a feeling that Danny ought to be labled a Judas, but I think that one thing that no one will forget is that Danny Wilson helped Barnsley Football Club create a piece of its own history.
Fan: Danny Wilson's a good manager, he's done a lot for the club, I wish he'd have stayed.

IAN
I went down the ground
The day after Wilson went
And the wind and the rain
Just wouldn't relent
And I was soaking wet
And I looked around
At the beautiful, hopeful Oakwell ground.

Samba Band play Just Like Watching Brazil

OLD MAN
So we start again
Division One
And we, the fans keep singing
And the song goes on
And at the end of next season, well, we shall see…
Whatever, I'll still be there, believe you me!

IAN
And football's like a river

GIRL
Football never ends

OLD MAN
And we will still be here

IAN
Whatever history sends

GIRL
The season starts again

OLD MAN
The sun defeats the rain

IAN
The carnival is swinging
And the pleasure kills the pain

CHORUS
Football looks back to the glory that's been
And on to the glory to come
And the moment of the game
Is a dazzling thing
Like staring too long at the sun
Like staring too long at the sun